HARRIET TUBMAN

Born in 1820

SUSAN B. ANTHONY

Julie Knutson

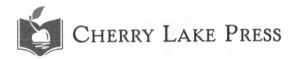
CHERRY LAKE PRESS

Published in the United States of America by Cherry Lake Publishing
Ann Arbor, Michigan
www.cherrylakepublishing.com

Reading Adviser: Marla Conn, MS, Ed., Literacy specialist, Read-Ability, Inc.
Cover Designer: Felicia Macheske

Photo Credits: © Library of Congress/Benjamin F. Powelson/www.loc.gov/item/2018645050/, cover, 1 [left]; © Library of Congress/C. M. Bell/www.loc.gov/item/2016689513/, cover, 2 [right]; © Marzolino/Shutterstock.com, 5; © Library of Congress, LC-DIG-ppmsca-52069, 6; © Lemon_tm/iStock.com, 9; © Library of Congress, LC-USZ62-75975, 10; © Library of Congress, LC-DIG-ppmsca-54232, 12; © Everett Historical/Shutterstock.com, 15, 19; © Leigh Prather/Shutterstock.com, 16; © Library of Congress, LC-DIG-ggbain-12783, 21; © Library of Congress, 159001u, 22; © Library of Congress, 160038u, 24; © Library of Congress, LC-DIG-hec-12120, 25; © Library of Congress, LC-DIG-ggbain-26590, 26

Library of Congress Cataloging-in-Publication Data

Names: Knutson, Julie, author.
Title: Born in 1820 : Harriet Tubman and Susan B. Anthony / by Julie Knutson.
Description: Ann Arbor, Michigan : Cherry Lake Publishing, [2020] | Series: Parallel lives | Includes bibliographical references and index. | Audience: Grades: 4-6
Identifiers: LCCN 2019033400 (print) | LCCN 2019033401 (ebook) | ISBN 9781534159167 (hardcover) | ISBN 9781534161467 (paperback) | ISBN 9781534160316 (pdf) | ISBN 9781534162617 (ebook)
Subjects: LCSH: Tubman, Harriet, 1822-1913—Juvenile literature. | Anthony, Susan B. (Susan Brownell), 1820-1906—Juvenile literature. | Women social reformers—United States—Biography—Juvenile literature. | Slaves—United States—Biography—Juvenile literature. | African American women—Biography—Juvenile literature. | Underground Railroad—Juvenile literature. | Feminists—United States—Biography—Juvenile literature. | Suffragists—United States—Biography—Juvenile literature. | Women's rights—United States—History—Juvenile literature.
Classification: LCC E444.T82 K63 2020 (print) | LCC E444.T82 (ebook) | DDC 326/.8092 [B]—dc23
LC record available at https://lccn.loc.gov/2019033400
LC ebook record available at https://lccn.loc.gov/2019033401

Cherry Lake Publishing would like to acknowledge the work of the Partnership for 21st Century Learning, a Network of Battelle for Kids. Please visit www.battelleforkids.org/networks/p21 for more information.

Printed in the United States of America
Corporate Graphics

ABOUT THE AUTHOR

Julie Knutson shares a birth year with Venus Williams, Chelsea Clinton, and Lin-Manuel Miranda. An avid student of history and former teacher, she lives in northern Illinois with her husband and son.

TABLE OF CONTENTS

CHAPTER 1

Welcome to 1820

1820. While the exact date is unknown, social reformer Harriet Tubman is born into slavery on Maryland's Eastern Shore. On February 15, 1820, another future activist, Susan B. Anthony, is born near Adams, Massachusetts. Over the course of their lives, these women worked to change the country into which they were born. Their shared goal was to make it more just for *all* people, regardless of color, social class, or gender.

Slavery: In 1820, there were 11 free states and 11 slave states in the United States. The issue of slavery was widely debated. Slaveholding interests in the South resisted as **abolitionism** gained momentum. The debate reached a turning point with the

The United States made it illegal to import new slaves in 1808.

Sojourner Truth escaped to freedom in 1826. She spoke out on rights for women and African Americans.

Missouri Compromise. The Missouri Territory was poised to join the Union as a slave state, which would tip the balance of power in Congress. To counter that imbalance, Maine was also granted statehood as a free state. It was agreed that future states admitted to the Union lying north of latitude 36°30' on a map would be free. Those below 36°30' would be slave states.

Women's Issues: In the 1820s, middle- and upper-middle class white women were expected to behave a certain way. They dwelled in the "separate **sphere**" of the household, while men participated in public life. A 19th-century girl's education largely involved training to be a wife and mother. Skills like sewing, home remedies, and household management were the curriculum. Middle- and upper-middle class girls might also study poetry, literature, history, and politics, but this knowledge would never be applied in the public sphere. For enslaved people, male or female, education was illegal.

Standing Together

*Throughout their lives, Harriet Tubman and Susan B. Anthony worked together on behalf of the shared causes of abolition and women's **suffrage**. Susan even introduced Harriet at the 1904 meeting at New York State for the National American Woman Suffrage Association. The two friends held hands during Susan's introduction to Harriet's speech.*

CHAPTER 2

Harriet Tubman
(b. ca. 1820)

Harriet Tubman wasn't afraid to take risks. In 1849—alone, on foot, and without any map to guide her—she fled life as an enslaved woman in Maryland. But she was concerned for the safety of family members still living under slavery. She later risked the freedom that she'd so daringly obtained and embarked on an estimated 12 to 19 secret rescue missions. Harriet fought against slavery through her actions *and* with her voice. She also took up other causes for justice, particularly women's rights, throughout her long life.

Harriet walked about 90 miles (145 kilometers) on her first trip to freedom.

Harriet sang coded songs to help lead slaves through the Underground Railroad.

Early Years: Finding a Voice

Harriet was born into slavery around 1820. In her early years, she lost part of her family when two sisters were sold to plantations farther south. Determined that this would never again happen, her mother hid Harriet's brother to prevent his sale at auction. At age 5, Harriet was sent to work as a **domestic** servant. There, she was expected to care for a newborn baby. Her white mistress whipped her as a warning to work hard. Sixty years later, Harriet still bore the scars from those lashings.

[21ST CENTURY SKILLS LIBRARY]

In her early teens, Harriet moved from housework to fieldwork. As a young adult, she suffered a massive head injury at the hands of an **overseer**. The overseer struck her with a heavy metal object, fracturing her skull and causing heavy bleeding. As a result of the injury, for the remainder of her life, Harriet suffered episodes where she would lose consciousness.

In 1844, she married a free black man, John Tubman. Marriage to a free man didn't give her any new rights. Harriet was still

What was the Underground Railroad?

The Underground Railroad was neither underground nor was it a railroad. It was actually a set of secret routes and safehouses that allowed enslaved blacks to reach freedom in the North and in Canada. A **clandestine** network of abolitionists—black and white—assisted in this quest for freedom. Because it operated in secrecy and largely by word of mouth, little is known about how and where it started.

What is known? Between 40,000 and 100,000 formerly enslaved people escaped via these routes, which spanned 14 Northern states, from Maine to Nebraska.

There was an award of $300 offered in the paper for the return of Harriet and her brothers.

enslaved, and any children that the couple bore would be considered the property of her owner. A few years later, in 1849, Harriet and two of her brothers escaped. They took flight, and a **bounty** was set for their capture. Out of fear of punishment, they returned. But Harriet wanted freedom, and she was willing to pursue it alone. A few weeks later, she fled north, leaving her husband and family behind. She was helped along her journey by a variety of people, many linked by a network known as the Underground Railroad.

Middle Years: Expressing a Voice

Harriet's journey to freedom ended in Philadelphia, Pennsylvania. In the late 1840s, the city was known for its thriving communities of abolitionist and free blacks. Harriet worked as a maid in hotels and social clubs to save money. She used these funds to finance return expeditions to Maryland to rescue other family members.

Philadelphia's status as a safe haven was short-lived. In 1850, the United States enacted the Fugitive Slave Act. This act stated that enslaved people captured in the North must be returned to their Southern owners. Harriet's focus shifted to leading enslaved people all the way to Canada, far north of the 36°30' line. She and her family relocated to St. Catharines, Ontario, in 1851, and she continued—by boat, foot, train, and wagon—to lead dangerous rescue missions there until 1857. She also spoke out for abolitionism and women's suffrage, lecturing under an **alias** to hide from slave catchers in the North.

Harriet continued her Underground Railroad work into the early 1860s. But in 1861, the Civil War broke out. She took on new roles in the service of the Union cause, working as a field nurse, cook, spy, and scout. The Union army tapped her knowledge of secret networks and routes to spy on the Confederacy. On June 2, 1863, she led the Combahee Ferry Raid in South Carolina. During this **covert** operation, she and 150 African American Union soldiers rescued more than 700 slaves. It was the largest **liberation** of enslaved people in U.S. history.

African American infantries played a key role in the
Union victory during the Civil War.

Harriet was buried with military honors.

Later Years: Leaving a Legacy

Harriet rescued and relocated nearly all of her family members, and countless others, in her decade as a conductor on the Underground Railroad. After the Civil War and her husband's death, she married Civil War veteran Nelson Davis. In her later years, Harriet settled in Auburn, New York. She continued speaking out for women's rights, raised money for African American schools, and built a home for elderly African Americans in need. In 1913, Harriet died in Auburn at age 93. She was buried with military honors. Today, she is still celebrated as an American who risked her own life—and shared her own experiences—to ensure the freedom and liberty of others.

"The Moses of Her People"

Inspired by the biblical story, abolitionist William Lloyd Garrison gave Harriet Tubman the nickname "Moses." Garrison paralleled Moses's deliverance of the Israelites from enslavement to Harriet's work to free enslaved Africans in the United States.

CHAPTER 3

Susan B. Anthony
(b. February 15, 1820)

"Failure is impossible." These are the last words that social reformer Susan B. Anthony spoke in public. As one who devoted her life to women's suffrage, Susan endured bullying, arrest, and violence for the sake of her cause. While she didn't live to see the **ratification** of the 19th Amendment in 1920, she shaped the path for its passage. With her message of "failure is impossible" and the movement she launched, she created a means for future activists to see the dream of full suffrage to reality.

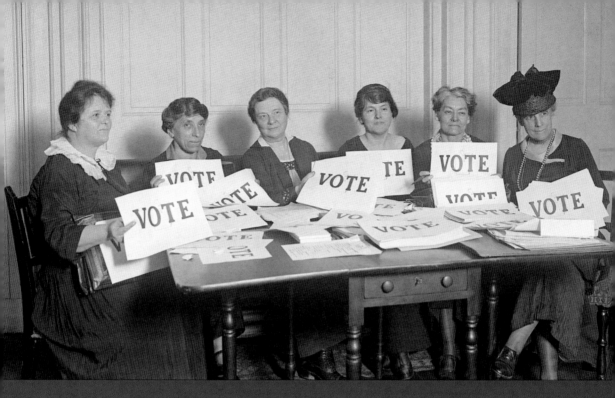

Quakers supported both the abolitionist movement and women's suffrage.

Early Years: Finding a Voice

Susan grew up in a household that rejected 19th-century ideas about gender and ability. Born into a **Quaker** family that stressed **integrity**, equality, and simplicity, she and her sisters received an education equal to their brothers. The outspoken young Susan wouldn't settle for less. While attending the local school near their home in Battenville, New York, the instructor refused to teach her long division. According to the teacher, it wasn't a skill girls needed. Susan thought otherwise. She persisted and taught herself. Her father, Daniel, supported her, pulling her out of the school. Daniel then started a private school for Susan and other local children at the Anthony family home.

Although most 19th-century girls didn't have the chance to pursue higher education, Susan continued her studies. In 1837, she was sent to boarding school in Pennsylvania. Her time there was cut short due to a nationwide financial panic, in which her previously well-off family lost nearly everything. Susan needed to earn income and began working as a teacher. She also helped manage the family farm near Rochester, New York. As she spent more time with her father and his abolitionist friends, she learned more about contemporary social justice concerns. Nearby events like the Seneca Falls Convention on women's rights in 1848 captured her attention. A couple years later, a chance meeting with one of the convention's organizers, Elizabeth Cady Stanton, helped Susan direct her belief in equality into informed action.

The Seneca Falls Convention was the first convention on women's rights in the United States.

Susan B. Anthony and Elizabeth Cady Stanton worked as a team.

Middle Years: Expressing a Voice

Susan and Elizabeth's friendship sparked a strong, sustained effort to gain women's rights. Like many of their contemporaries, they saw connections between the rights of women and those of enslaved peoples. They jointly pursued civil rights for both oppressed groups. **Temperance** was another cause that reformers rallied around. Women's rights supporters wanted to establish the legal right to divorce drunk and violent husbands. In her early activist years, Susan spoke out and organized on behalf of all of these causes.

After the Civil War, Susan and Elizabeth expected the newly introduced civil rights amendments to the U.S. Constitution—which related to citizenship and voting rights—to apply to *all* Americans, regardless of race or gender. They didn't. These laws exclusively applied to men. The pair then focused all their energies on extending those same rights to women. They published a newspaper, *The Revolution*, to advance their views. They spoke in public. And they acted. In 1872, Susan insisted on her constitutional

Women's Suffrage by State

Different U.S. territories and states granted women the right to vote at different times in history. Wyoming Territory was the first, extending full suffrage in 1869.

Other women were also arrested for voting, but Susan was the only one who went to trial.

right to vote at a polling station in New York. She was arrested. While she hoped that the U.S. Supreme Court would take up her case, the government declined to pursue the matter.

Despite such setbacks, Susan and Elizabeth continued in their efforts. Between 1869 and 1906, Susan appeared before every U.S. Congress to **lobby** for women's voting rights. In 1878, a measure to extend suffrage to women was first introduced. It was known as the Susan B. Anthony Amendment. While some states passed laws allowing women to vote, it wasn't until 1919 that this amendment was formally passed. It was ratified in 1920.

The passage of the 19th Amendment came down to one vote. The tie-breaking representative was convinced by a letter his mother wrote him.

In the 1920 elections, there were 8 million more votes cast than in the previous election. Many people attribute this to the passage of the 19th Amendment.

Later Years: Leaving a Legacy

Equal education for girls, equal pay for women, and gender equality before the law were all issues put on the political table by Susan in the mid-19th century. Her tireless work for women's rights has been **commemorated** on everything from coins to postage stamps. Susan's advice was to "think your best thoughts, speak your best words, do your best works, looking to your own conscience for approval." Her words continue to inspire civil rights activists, 100 years after the ratification of the amendment that bears her name.

Women on U.S. Currency

In 2016, the U.S. Department of the Treasury announced that Harriet Tubman would replace Andrew Jackson on the $20 bill. Set for release in 2020, the new bill would coincide with the 100th anniversary of the 19th Amendment. On its release, Tubman would join five other women who have previously appeared on U.S. currency: Pocahontas, Martha Washington, Sacagawea, Helen Keller, and Susan B. Anthony.

In 2019, Treasury Secretary Steven Mnuchin announced that the bill featuring Tubman would be delayed for several years due to security reasons. Some experts note that the design process for the new bill was quite advanced, so many critics have questioned if the decision was politically motivated.

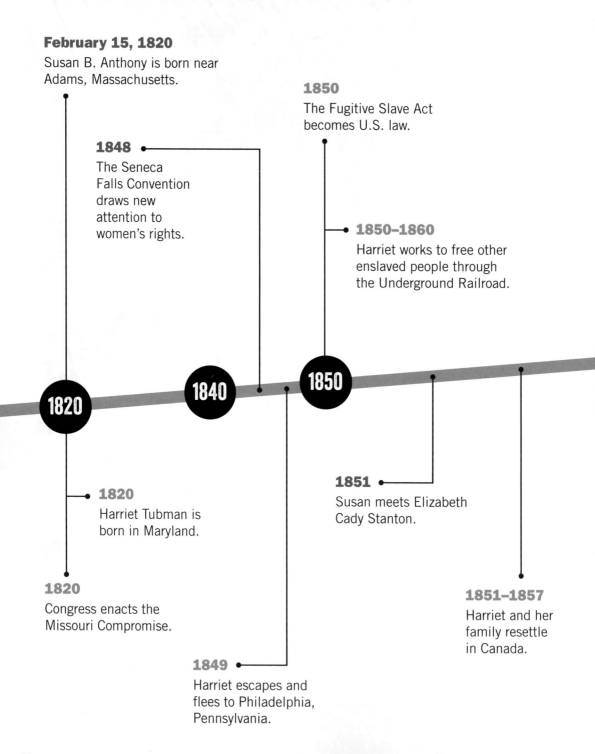

February 15, 1820
Susan B. Anthony is born near Adams, Massachusetts.

1850
The Fugitive Slave Act becomes U.S. law.

1848
The Seneca Falls Convention draws new attention to women's rights.

1850–1860
Harriet works to free other enslaved people through the Underground Railroad.

1820

1840

1850

1820
Harriet Tubman is born in Maryland.

1851
Susan meets Elizabeth Cady Stanton.

1820
Congress enacts the Missouri Compromise.

1851–1857
Harriet and her family resettle in Canada.

1849
Harriet escapes and flees to Philadelphia, Pennsylvania.

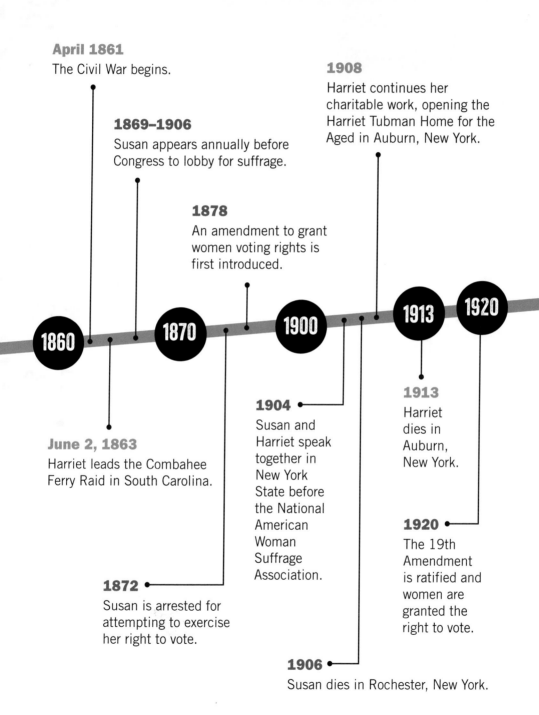

April 1861
The Civil War begins.

1869–1906
Susan appears annually before Congress to lobby for suffrage.

1908
Harriet continues her charitable work, opening the Harriet Tubman Home for the Aged in Auburn, New York.

1878
An amendment to grant women voting rights is first introduced.

1860

1870

1900

1913

1920

June 2, 1863
Harriet leads the Combahee Ferry Raid in South Carolina.

1904
Susan and Harriet speak together in New York State before the National American Woman Suffrage Association.

1913
Harriet dies in Auburn, New York.

1872
Susan is arrested for attempting to exercise her right to vote.

1920
The 19th Amendment is ratified and women are granted the right to vote.

1906
Susan dies in Rochester, New York.

Research and Act

Artist Jacob Lawrence paid tribute to Harriet Tubman in a series of 31 paintings. Each of them highlights a significant event in her life. Lawrence was inspired to create the series by the stories he had learned about her growing up.

Research

What historical figure has made an impact on you? What more would you like to learn about him or her? Research their life. Make a timeline of key events and turning points in their personal history.

Act

Do as Lawrence did! Memorialize this person in a series of images of your own. The form can vary from cartoons or collages to paintings or drawings. Share your work with family and friends to communicate why this person matters to you and how they shaped history.

Further Reading

Chambers, Veronica. *Resist: 35 Profiles of Ordinary People Who Rose Up Against Tyranny and Injustice.* New York, NY: Harper, 2018.

Kanefield, Teri. *Susan B. Anthony.* New York, NY: Abrams Books for Young Readers, 2019.

Krasner, Barbara. *Harriet Tubman: Abolitionist and Conductor of the Underground Railroad.* New York, NY: Britannica Educational Publishing, in association with Rosen Educational Services, 2018.

McDonough, Yona Zeldis. *Who Was Harriet Tubman?* New York, NY: Grosset & Dunlap, 2002.

Pollack, Pamela D. *Who Was Susan B. Anthony?* New York, NY: Grosset & Dunlap, 2014.

GLOSSARY

abolitionism (ab-uh-LISH-uh-niz-um) organized 19th-century movement to end slavery

alias (AY-lee-uhs) an alternate name

bounty (BOUN-tee) a reward

clandestine (klan-DES-tin) in secret

commemorated (kuh-MEM-uh-rate-id) honored and remembered a person because they were important

covert (KOH-vurt) in secret or private

domestic (duh-MES-tik) having to do with the home

integrity (in-TEG-rih-tee) being honest and morally upright

liberation (lib-uh-RAY-shuhn) the act of freeing someone from slavery or prison

lobby (LAH-bee) to try to influence a politician or public official

overseer (OH-vur-see-ur) supervisor of workers

Quaker (KWAY-kur) a Christian group that prefers simple religious services and opposes war

ratification (rat-uh-fih-KAY-shuhn) the process of making a law official

sphere (SFEER) area of activity, interest, or knowledge

suffrage (SUHF-rij) right to vote

temperance (TEM-pruhns) a movement to ban alcohol consumption

INDEX

[21ST CENTURY SKILLS LIBRARY]